No. _____

In the
Supreme Court of the United States

DEADRIA FARMER-PAELLMANN, ET AL.,

Petitioners,

v.

SMITHSONIAN INSTITUTION,

Respondent.

**On Petition for a Writ of Certiorari to the
United States Court of Appeals for the District of Columbia**

PETITION FOR A WRIT OF CERTIORARI

Bruce I. Afran
Counsel of Record
10 Braeburn Dr.
Princeton, NJ 08540
(609) 454-7435
bruceafran@aol.com

May 28, 2024

Counsel for Petitioner

SUPREME COURT PRESS ♦ (888) 958-5705 ♦ BOSTON, MASSACHUSETTS

QUESTIONS PRESENTED

1. Whether subject matter jurisdiction exists over the Smithsonian Institution's repatriation of artworks to a foreign state under an Ethical Return policy without using the rulemaking and public hearing processes under the Administrative Procedure Act, (APA), 5 U.S.C. § 552a, *et seq*.

2. Whether descendants of enslaved Africans in the United States have Article III standing to challenge the repatriation by the Smithsonian Institution of 29 of the "Benin Bronzes", artworks that were formed out of the metal ingots used by western slave traders to purchase enslaved persons from the Kingdom of Benin.

3. Whether the courts below improperly held the matter to be moot where nine of the Benin Bronzes had title transferred by the Smithsonian to Nigeria but remain in the United States on long-term loan, along with other Bronzes still in U.S. title but subject to future repatriation.

PARTIES TO THE PROCEEDINGS

Petitioners and Plaintiffs-Appellants below

- Deadria Farmer-Paellmann
- Restitution Study Group, Inc

Respondent and Plaintiff-Appellees below

- Smithsonian Institution

STATEMENT PURSUANT TO SUPREME COURT RULE 29.6

Petitioner Restitution Study Group, Inc. is a privately-owned entity. It has no parent corporation and there is no publicly held company that owns 10% or more of their stock.

LIST OF PROCEEDINGS

U.S. Court of Appeals, District of Columbia Circuit

No. 23-5196

Deadria Farmer-Paellmann and Restitution Study Group, Inc., *Appellants* v. Smithsonian Institution, *Appellee*

Date of Final Order: December 28, 2023

Date of Rehearing Denial: February 29, 2024

U.S. District Court, District of Columbia

No. 22-cv-3048 (CRC)

Deadria Farmer-Paellmann, et al., *Plaintiffs*, v. Smithsonian Institution, *Defendant*.

Date of Final Opinion: July 5, 2023

TABLE OF CONTENTS

	Page
QUESTIONS PRESENTED	i
PARTIES TO THE PROCEEDINGS	ii
STATEMENT PURSUANT TO SUPREME COURT RULE 29.6	iii
LIST OF PROCEEDINGS	iv
TABLE OF AUTHORITIES	vii
OPINIONS BELOW	1
JURISDICTION	1
JUDICIAL RULES INVOLVED	2
STATEMENT OF THE CASE	2
REASONS FOR GRANTING THE PETITION	6
CONCLUSION	9

TABLE OF CONTENTS – Continued

Page

APPENDIX TABLE OF CONTENTS

OPINIONS AND ORDERS

Order Under R. 36, U.S. Court of Appeals for the D.C. Circuit (December 28, 2023) 1a

Memorandum Opinion, U.S. District Court for the District of Columbia (July 5, 2023) 3a

Order Dismissing Case, U.S. District Court for the District of Columbia (July 5, 2023) 7a

Opinion and Order Denying Emergency Temporary Restraining Order, U.S. District Court for the District of Columbia (October 14, 2022) 9a

REHEARING ORDER

Order Denying Petition for Rehearing, U.S. Court of Appeals for the D.C. Circuit (February 29, 2024) 13a

OTHER DOCUMENTS

Complaint (October 7, 2022) 15a

Emergency Motion for TRO and Preliminary Injunction (October 7, 2022) 39a

Contract Between Smithsonian Institution and Nigerian National Commission for Museums and Monuments (October 11, 2022) 41a

TABLE OF AUTHORITIES

Page

CASES

Aetna Life Insurance Co. v. Haworth,
  300 U.S. 227 (1937) 8

Allen v. Wright,
  468 U.S. 737 (1984) 8

Baker v. Carr,
  369 U.S. 186 (1962) 8

Colhoun v. Smithsonian Inst.,
  659 F.Supp. 1551 (D. Md. 1987) 6

Crowley v. Smithsonian Inst.,
  462 F. Supp. 725 (D.D.C. 1978) 6

Dong v. Smithsonian Inst.,
  125 F.3d 877 (D.C. Cir. 1997) 5, 6

Lewis v. Continental Bank Corp.,
  494 U.S. 472 (1990) 8

Los Angeles v. Lyons,
  461 U.S. 95 (1983) 8

NCUA v. First Nat'l Bank & Trust Co.,
  522 U.S. 479 (1998) 7

Norden v. Samper,
  503 F.Supp.2d 130 (D.D.C. 2007) 6

O'Rourke v. Smithsonian Inst. Press,
  399 F.3d 113 (2d Cir. 2005) 6

Valley Forge Christian College v. Americans United for Separation of Church & State, Inc., 454 U.S. 464 (1982) 8

Williams v. Smithsonian Inst.,
  177 F.Supp.3d 377 (D.D.C. 2016) 6

TABLE OF AUTHORITIES – Continued

Page

CONSTITUTIONAL PROVISIONS

U.S. Const. amend. I 7

U.S. Const. art. III .... i, 8

STATUTES

28 U.S.C. § 1254 1

28 U.S.C. § 2101 1

5 U.S.C. § 551(1) 6

5 U.S.C. § 552(f) 6

5 U.S.C. § 702.5 5

Administrative Procedure Act,
    5 U.S.C. § 552a, *et seq* .... i, 3, 4, 5, 8

Rehabilitation Act of 1973 6

JUDICIAL RULES

Fed. R. Civ. P. Rule 12(b)(1) 2

Fed. R. Civ. P. Rule 12(b)(6) 2

Sup. Ct. R. 13.1 1

Sup. Ct. R. 29.6 iii

OTHER AUTHORITIES

U.S. Mission Nigeria,
    30 Benin Bronzes Returned to Nigeria
    (Oct. 17, 2022), https://ng.usembassy.gov/
    30-benin-bronzes-returned-to-nigeria/ 4, 5

OPINIONS BELOW

The ruling of the United States Court of Appeals for the D.C. Circuit dated December 28, 2023 granting summary affirmance of the decision of the District Court is included in the Appendix ("App.") at 1a. The memorandum decision of the United States District Court for the District of Columbia, dated July 5, 2023 is included at App.3a.

JURISDICTION

The United States Court of Appeals for the District of Columbia Circuit denied a timely petition for rehearing on February 29, 2024 which is included at App.13a. U.S. Court of Appeals for the D.C. Circuit. This petition is timely under 28 U.S.C. § 2101 and Supreme Court Rule 13.1 because it is being filed within 90 days of the entry of the order sought to be reviewed. This court has jurisdiction to review the order of the United States Court of Appeals for the Second Circuit pursuant to 28 U.S.C. § 1254.

JUDICIAL RULES INVOLVED

The relevant provision of the Federal Rules of Civil Procedure is Fed. R. Civ. P. 12(b)(1) and (6).

Fed. R. Civ. P. Rule 12. (b)(1), (6)

Defenses and Objections: When and How Presented; Motion for Judgment on the Pleadings; Consolidating Motions; Waiving Defenses; Pretrial Hearing

[. . .]

(b) How to Present Defenses. Every defense to a claim for relief in any pleading must be asserted in the responsive pleading if one is required. But a party may assert the following defenses by motion:

(1) lack of subject-matter jurisdiction;

[. . .]

(6) failure to state a claim upon which relief can be granted;

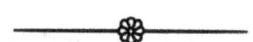

STATEMENT OF THE CASE

Smithsonian Institution (Smithsonian) has engaged in the creation of a federal repatriation policy to return artworks, namely the Benin Bronzes (the Bronzes), to a foreign state. In so doing, Smithsonian has acted unilaterally and outside of any regulation under the Administrative Procedure Act (APA), 5 U.S.C. § 552a, *et seq.*

Under what it calls the "Shared Stewardship and Ethical Return Policy" (the "Ethical Return policy"), Smithsonian has transferred title to 29 Benin Bronzes, the well-known sculptural masks created in what was once the Benin Kingdom, now a part of Nigeria. The Bronzes were removed by Britain in 1897 during its colonial administration of Benin and found their way to various institutions, including Smithsonian. Of the twenty-nine (29) Bronzes, twenty (20) were moved to Nigeria during the District Court action while the remaining nine (9) had title transferred to Nigeria but remain in the U.S. under a nine-year "loan" to Smithsonian. App.43a-46a.

The District Court held that the matter was moot despite plaintiffs' claims that as to the nine Bronzes remaining in the U.S. a remedy could still be effected reversing the transfer of title. In addition, plaintiffs argued that approximately Forty (40) more Bronzes remain in the Smithsonian and can still be made subject to the Ethical Return policy, giving rise to a continuing ripe controversy. The lower courts rejected both claims to ripeness. App.2a, App.4a.

The District Court also held that Smithsonian was not obligated or subject to the APA and did not have to provide a public forum prior to its adoption of the Ethical Return policy and that plaintiffs lacked standing to raise such issues. App.10a.

In the District Court, Smithsonian made it clear that the repatriation of the Bronzes was a governmental policy, going so far as to tell the District Court that interference with the transfer "would vitiate a contract *between two sovereign nations*." Government Response at 19 [emphasis added]. In this same vein, Smithsonian told the District Court it had "entered into an agreement with an arm of the Nigerian government," *id.* at 20, and that plaintiffs should not be permitted to "disturb an agreement *between sovereign nations* to return home antiquities originating in Nigeria." *Id.* [emphasis added] By such concessions, Smithsonian acknowledged it created a governmental policy but one that was implemented without recourse to the rule-making provisions of the APA.

In execution of the repatriation, the U.S. Department of State viewed the return of the Bronzes as an official act, placing the return within the context of a January 2022 agreement between the United States and Nigeria to prevent the looting and trafficking of Nigeria's cultural property. *See* U.S. Mission Nigeria, *30 Benin Bronzes Returned to Nigeria* (Oct. 17, 2022), https://ng.usembassy.gov/30-benin-bronzes-returned-to-nigeria/.[1]

Repatriation was also treated as a diplomatic act. Nigeria's Minister of Education and Culture, Lai Mohammed, attended the transfer of ownership ceremony at the National Museum of African Art on October 11, 2022. Moreover, the U.S. embassy high-

---

[1] Notably, that "agreement" does not authorize Smithsonian to engage in any repatriation of the U.S. collection and speaks only to aspirations between the two governments to fight art object trafficking. Smithsonian should still have made use of the APA to create the repatriation policy since it is plainly a new governmental initiative. Even if it were authorized under a Congressional mandate, the nature of the repatriation program would ordinarily require resort to the APA and its public hearing processes.

lighted the repatriation on its website. *See* U.S. Mission Nigeria, *30 Benin Bronzes Returned to Nigeria* (Oct. 17, 2022), https://ng.usembassy.gov/30-benin-bronzes-returned-to-nigeria/.[2]

By every reasonable measure, Smithsonian's repatriation of the Bronzes has been treated as national policy but Smithsonian contends it was not subject to the APA or any federal jurisdiction in the creation of what amounts to a federal art repatriation initiative, a shocking aggregation of agency power.

Citing a Privacy Act case, the District Court agreed with Smithsonian and held, in part, that it had no subject matter jurisdiction because Smithsonian is not an "agency" under the APA and there is no basis for judicial review under 5 U.S.C. § 702.5. App.10a (citing *Dong v. Smithsonian Inst.*, 125 F.3d 877, 883 (D.C. Cir. 1997)).

Congress never authorized repatriation to a foreign state by *any* agency, let alone Smithsonian that is a trustee of the United States collection. In creating what amounts to federal policy, Smithsonian should be deemed subject to the APA and create such policy only by public hearings and the public rule-making process. In the absence of such public process, the Ethical Return policy and decisions based upon the policy are *ultra vires* and should be deemed void.

---

[2] Nigeria's President also recognized the repatriation as a governmental act in a proclamation dated March 23, 2023 headed "Recognition of Ownership, and an Order Vesting Custody and Management of the Repatriated Looted Benin Artifacts in the Oba of Benin Kingdom, 2023." (Ex. 2), https://dailysceptic.org/wp-content/uploads/2023/05/2023-03-28-re-Oba-Federal-Republic-Of-Nigeria-Official-Gazette.pdf.

These claims were novel and required extended argument but the Court of Appeals dismissed the appeal on all issues by a truncated and highly limited summary affirmance. App.1a.

REASONS FOR GRANTING THE PETITION

Despite the evidence of a new policy initiative, the District Court held that Smithsonian is not an agency exercising the "authority of the government of the United States" under § 551(1) and lacks the executive department status necessary under § 552(f) to engage the mandatory APA public process. App.10a, *citing Dong, supra* at 882-883. However, such assumption is not absolute and Smithsonian falls under federal judicial authority when the *factual* basis of its acts give rise to jurisdiction. *See e.g. O'Rourke v. Smithsonian Inst. Press*, 399 F.3d 113 (2d Cir. 2005) (holding that Smithsonian is considered "the United States" in the context of copyright infringement).[3]

---

[3] District Courts have not hesitated to recognize jurisdiction over Smithsonian in a variety of factual contexts. *Williams v. Smithsonian Inst.*, 177 F.Supp.3d 377 (D.D.C. 2016) (denying motion to dismiss employee's retaliation claim); *Norden v. Samper*, 503 F.Supp.2d 130 (D.D.C. 2007) (granting summary judgment against Smithsonian Institution for failure to accommodate an employee's handicap under the Rehabilitation Act of 1973 and retaliation in firing the employee); *Colhoun v. Smithsonian Inst.*, 659 F.Supp. 1551 (D. Md. 1987) (asserting jurisdiction over claim against Smithsonian for specific performance of an option agreement); *Crowley v. Smithsonian Inst.*, 462 F. Supp. 725 (D.D.C. 1978) (denying a claim under the U.S. Constitution's Establishment Clause that the Smithsonian's exhibits on the sub-

In connection with the Benin Bronzes, Smithsonian has exercised the "authority of the United States" via what Smithsonian admitted below is an agreement "between sovereign nations"; as such, Smithsonian should have had resort to the APA process and its public participation component, an important element of speech and redress under the First Amendment. The lower courts erred by failing to recognize the factual distinction between the Smithsonian's ordinary function as a museum and its policymaking innovation in the form of repatriation of the Bronzes.

In the complaint below, plaintiffs asserted historical, cultural, aesthetic, and symbolic interests that are peculiar to plaintiff Farmer-Paellmann and Restitution Study Group that advocate for the collective interests of descendants of enslaved Africans. App.16a-17a, 19a-24a, 35a-37a. Plaintiffs fall within "the zone of interests", *see e.g. NCUA v. First Nat'l Bank & Trust Co.*, 522 U.S. 479, 492 (1998), of descendants of enslaved Africans to claim standing to object to the removal of the Bronzes that have symbolic meaning, having been created out of the metal ingots used by western slave traders as the currency to purchase Africans from the Benin kingdom.

A symbolic tie exists between the Bronzes and descendants of enslaved persons so as to create a nexus with the Smithsonian's decision to "repatriate" the Bronzes. Since the Ethical Return policy remains in force and has not been revoked, these plaintiffs continue to have a "'personal stake in the outcome'" of the

---

ject of evolution were outside its statutory authority and violated the First Amendment).

lawsuit. *Los Angeles v. Lyons*, 461 U.S. 95, 101 (1983) (quoting *Baker v. Carr*, 369 U.S. 186, 204 (1962)).

Plaintiffs demonstrated sufficient Article III standing to seek injunctive relief to reverse title in the nine Bronzes still in the U.S. and to seek declaratory relief as to the others (approximately 40) subject to future invocation of the Ethical Return policy. *See e.g. Lewis v. Continental Bank Corp.*, 494 U.S. 472, 477 (1990); *Allen v. Wright*, 468 U.S. 737, 750-751 (1984); *Valley Forge Christian College v. Americans United for Separation of Church & State, Inc.*, 454 U.S. 464, 471-473 (1982). Plaintiffs presented a real and not "a hypothetical state of facts."' *Cf. Aetna Life Insurance Co. v. Haworth*, 300 U.S. 227, 241 (1937)).

Finally, by limiting its summary affirmance solely to the mootness question, App.1a-2a, the Court of Appeals failed to consider the important policy questions presented by plaintiffs as to Smithsonian's creation of federal policy without resort to the public hearing process under the APA.

CONCLUSION

The Petition for a Writ of Certiorari should be granted.

Respectfully submitted,

Bruce I. Afran
  Counsel of Record
10 Braeburn Dr.
Princeton, NJ 08540
(609) 454-7435
bruceafran@aol.com

Counsel for Petitioner

May 28, 2024

APPENDIX TABLE OF CONTENTS

OPINIONS AND ORDERS

Order Under R. 36, U.S. Court of Appeals
    for the D.C. Circuit (December 28, 2023) 1a

Memorandum Opinion, U.S. District Court
    for the District of Columbia (July 5, 2023) 3a

Order Dismissing Case, U.S. District Court
    for the District of Columbia (July 5, 2023) 7a

Opinion and Order Denying Emergency
    Temporary Restraining Order,
    U.S. District Court for the District of
    Columbia (October 14, 2022) 9a

REHEARING ORDER

Order Denying Petition for Rehearing,
    U.S. Court of Appeals for the D.C. Circuit
    (February 29, 2024) 13a

OTHER DOCUMENTS

Complaint
    (October 7, 2022) 15a

Emergency Motion for TRO and Preliminary
    Injunction (October 7, 2022) 39a

Contract Between Smithsonian Institution and
    Nigerian National Commission for Museums
    and Monuments (October 11, 2022) 41a

App.1a

ORDER UNDER R. 36, U.S. COURT OF APPEALS FOR THE D.C. CIRCUIT (DECEMBER 28, 2023)

UNITED STATES COURT OF APPEALS
FOR THE DISTRICT OF COLUMBIA CIRCUIT

DEADRIA FARMER-PAELLMANN AND RESTITUTION STUDY GROUP, INC.,

Appellants,

v.

SMITHSONIAN INSTITUTION,

Appellee.

No. 23-5196

1:22-cv-03048-CRC

Before: HENDERSON, CHILDS, and PAN, Circuit Judges.

ORDER

Upon consideration of the motion for summary affirmance, the opposition thereto, and the reply; and the motion for summary reversal, the opposition thereto, and the reply, it is

ORDERED that the motion for summary reversal be denied and that the motion for summary affirmance be granted. The merits of the parties' positions are so clear as to warrant summary action. *See Taxpayers Watchdog, Inc. v. Stanley*, 819 F.2d 294, 297 (D.C. Cir. 1987) (per curiam). Appellants have conceded certain points and forfeited various arguments concerning mootness. *See, e.g., District of Columbia v. Air Florida, Inc.*, 750 F.2d 1077, 1084 (D.C. Cir. 1984); *United States ex rel. Totten v. Bombardier Corp.*, 380 F.3d 488, 497 (D.C. Cir. 2004). Even without those concessions and forfeitures, appellants have not shown any error in the district court's holding that this case is moot in light of appellee's transfer of the ownership of 29 Benin Bronzes to Nigeria in October 2022. *See Lewis v. Continental Bank Corp.*, 494 U.S. 472, 477 (1990); *McBryde v. Committee to Review Circuit Council Conduct and Disability Orders*, 264 F.3d 52, 55 (D.C. Cir. 2001).

Pursuant to D.C. Circuit Rule 36, this disposition will not be published. The Clerk is directed to withhold issuance of the mandate herein until seven days after resolution of any timely petition for rehearing or petition for rehearing en banc. *See* Fed. R. App. P. 41(b); D.C. Cir. Rule 41.

Per Curiam

FOR THE COURT:

Mark J. Langer
Clerk

BY: /s/ Amy Yacisin
Deputy Clerk

MEMORANDUM OPINION, U.S. DISTRICT COURT FOR THE DISTRICT OF COLUMBIA (JULY 5, 2023)

UNITED STATES DISTRICT COURT
FOR THE DISTRICT OF COLUMBIA

DEADRIA FARMER-PAELLMANN, ET AL.,

Plaintiffs,

v.

SMITHSONIAN INSTITUTION,

Defendant.

Case No. 22-cv-3048 (CRC)

Before: Christopher R. COOPER,
United States District Judge.

MEMORANDUM OPINION

Plaintiffs, Deadria Farmer-Paellmann and Restitution Study Group, sought injunctive relief and, later, a temporary restraining order ("TRO") to prevent the Smithsonian Institution from repatriating a portion of its collection of artifacts known as the "Benin Bronzes" to a national museum in Nigeria. Plaintiffs alleged that transferring 29 of the 39 Benin Bronzes in the Smithsonian's collection would exceed its authority, breach the Smithsonian's trust relationships with the people of the United States and U.S. citizens of West African descent, and unjustly enrich the receiving museum. This Court denied the TRO request, finding that Plaintiffs were unlikely to succeed on their claims because they lacked standing, failed to assert any valid cause of action, and had not alleged that irreparable harm would occur if the Bronzes were transferred. Op. and Order, ECF No. 10, at 1, 3. Plaintiffs appealed, but withdrew the appeal and expressed intent to amend their complaint "in the next two weeks." Pls.' Notice of Withdrawal, ECF No. 13, at 1. Three months have passed, however, and Plaintiffs have yet to seek leave to file an amended complaint. The Court is left with Plaintiffs' original complaint seeking to enjoin the Smithsonian from transferring title of the Bronzes, which the Smithsonian moved to dismiss at the same time it opposed Plaintiffs' TRO request.[1] The motion is granted.

For myriad reasons, the Court lacks subject-matter jurisdiction to hear the case. *See Worth v. Jackson*, 451 F.3d 854, 857 (D.C. Cir. 2006) (explaining that "standing, mootness, and ripeness doctrines" establish the boundaries of the court's subject-matter jurisdiction). To start, Plaintiffs' claims now appear moot because title to the Bronzes has already been transferred.[2] Plaintiffs must retain a justiciable controversy throughout the litigation, and a case becomes moot "when it is impossible for a court to

---

[1] Plaintiffs opposed the motion to dismiss alongside their reply to the government's TRO opposition. *See* Pls.' Mem. in Opp'n to Mot. Dismiss, ECF No. 9.

[2] While the Smithsonian did not raise the issue of mootness in its motion to dismiss, which was filed before the transfer, the Court has "an independent obligation to determine whether subject-matter jurisdiction exists." *Arbaugh v. Y & H Corp.*, 546 U.S. 500, 514 (2006).

grant any effectual relief whatever to the prevailing party." *See Campbell-Ewald Co. v. Gomez,* 577 U.S. 153, 160–61 (2016). A moot case must be dismissed. *Id.* Here, Plaintiffs seek to permanently enjoin the Smithsonian from transferring title of the Bronzes. Compl. at 19–20. But as has been widely reported and officially confirmed by the U.S. government, the Smithsonian already transferred ownership of the 29 Benin Bronzes at issue on October 11, 2022.[3] *See, e.g.,* Kelsey Ables, *Smithsonian gives back 29 Benin bronzes to Nigeria: 'We are not owners',* Wash. Post (Oct. 11, 2022, 4:57 PM), *https://perma.cc/JJ5A-Q53A*; Michael Laff, *30 Benin Bronzes Returned to Nigeria,* U.S. Embassy and Consulate in Nigeria (Oct. 17, 2022), *https://perma.cc/62ZF-76AF*. Accordingly, there is no relief the Court can grant to Plaintiffs, so the case must be dismissed as moot.

Even if the Court interpreted the complaint broadly to avoid mootness issues, Plaintiffs still would lack standing to pursue their claims. To have standing, a plaintiff "must have suffered an injury in fact" that is "(a) concrete and particularized and (b) actual or imminent, not conjectural or hypothetical[.]" *Lujan v. Defs. of Wildlife,* 504 U.S. 555, 560 (1992) (cleaned up). Even assuming Plaintiffs intended to enjoin the Smithsonian from transferring the remaining ten Bronzes in its collection, there are no allegations to support that another transfer is "actual or imminent." Such an injury would be "too speculative" to support

---

[3] When analyzing subject-matter jurisdiction, the Court may consider materials outside the pleadings. *See Settles v. U.S. Parole Comm'n,* 429 F.3d 1098, 1107 (D.C. Cir. 2005).

standing. *See Clapper v. Amnesty Intern. USA*, 568 U.S. 398, 409 (2013).

Moreover, even if Plaintiffs have standing, they have failed to assert any valid causes of action to challenge the Smithsonian's decision to transfer the Bronzes, as the Court explained in its TRO ruling. Op. and Order, ECF No. 10, at 1. To recap, Plaintiffs' *ultra vires* claim fails because the Smithsonian is explicitly empowered to "transfer" works in its collection, 20 U.S.C. § 80m(a)(2); Plaintiffs' allegations about breaches of trust relationships falter because the "United States, as trustee, holds legal title to the original Smithson trust property and later accretions," not U.S. citizens or any subsection of U.S. citizens, *see Dong v. Smithsonian Inst.*, 125 F.3d 877, 883 (D.C. Cir. 1997); and Plaintiffs' unjust enrichment claim does not allege that the Smithsonian has received a benefit from the Plaintiffs without adequate compensation, *see Rapaport v. U.S. Dep't of Treasury, Off. of Thrift Supervision,* 59 F.3d 212, 217 (D.C. Cir. 1995).

The Court will, accordingly, grant Defendant's motion and dismiss the case.

A separate order will follow.

/s/ Christopher R. Cooper
United States District Judge

Date: July 5, 2023

App.7a

ORDER DISMISSING CASE, U.S. DISTRICT COURT FOR THE DISTRICT OF COLUMBIA (JULY 5, 2023)

UNITED STATES DISTRICT COURT
FOR THE DISTRICT OF COLUMBIA

DEADRIA FARMER-PAELLMANN, ET AL.,

Plaintiffs,

v.

SMITHSONIAN INSTITUTION,

Defendant.

Case No. 22-cv-3048 (CRC)

Before: Christopher R. COOPER,
United States District Judge.

ORDER

For the reasons stated in the accompanying Memorandum Opinion, it is hereby

ORDERED that [7] Defendant's Motion to Dismiss is GRANTED.

This is a final appealable Order.

SO ORDERED.

/s/ Christopher R. Cooper
United States District Judge

Date: July 5, 2023

OPINION AND ORDER DENYING EMERGENCY TEMPORARY RESTRAINING ORDER, U.S. DISTRICT COURT FOR THE DISTRICT OF COLUMBIA (OCTOBER 14, 2022)

UNITED STATES DISTRICT COURT
FOR THE DISTRICT OF COLUMBIA

DEADRIA FARMER-PAELLMANN, ET AL.,

Plaintiffs,

v.

SMITHSONIAN INSTITUTION,

Defendant.

Case No. 1:22-cv-3048 (CRC)

Before: Christopher R. COOPER,
United States District Judge.

OPINION AND ORDER

Plaintiffs, Deadria Farmer-Paellmann and Restitution Study Group, seek an emergency temporary restraining order to prevent the Smithsonian Institution from repatriating a portion of its collection of artifacts known as the "Benin Bronzes" to a national museum in Nigeria. The motion is denied.

Plaintiffs have not met their burden of showing they are likely to succeed on their claims because they appear to lack standing and have not asserted any valid cause of action to challenge the Smithsonian's decision to transfer some of the Bronzes.

Plaintiffs base standing on the assertion that they have a concrete personal stake in retaining access to the Bronzes because Ms. Farmer-Paellmann is a descendant of individuals who, between the 16th century and 19th century, were sold into slavery by the Kingdom of Benin in exchange for the metal that was used to fabricate the Bronzes. But even if Plaintiffs could establish that ancestral link to the Bronzes—which they have not done on this record—such an attenuated connection would not give rise to the type of "concrete and particularized" injury necessary for standing. *See Lujan v. Defenders of Wildlife*, 504 U.S. 555, 560 (1992).[1]

Plaintiffs are unlikely to succeed on the merits of any of their asserted claims even if they have standing. Plaintiffs' *ultra vires* claim fails because the Smithsonian's actions are not subject to judicial review under the Administrative Procedure Act. *See Dong v. Smithsonian Inst.*, 125 F.3d 877, 883 (D.C. Cir. 1997). In any event, the authorizing statute of the Smithsonian's Museum of African Art, where the Bronzes are held, explicitly empowers its Board to, among other things, "transfer" works in its collection. *See* 20 U.S.C. § 80m(a)(2). Accordingly, the Smithsonian does not appear to have acted beyond its statutory authority by reaching an agreement with Nigeria to transfer some of the Benin Bronzes.

---

[1] Plaintiffs might be able to establish standing based on a different injury, such as harm to an academic or aesthetic interest in the Bronzes, which might be heightened by their alleged ancestral ties, but they do not advance those arguments in any detail.

Plaintiffs' claims that the transfer would breach a trust relationship fare no better. While Plaintiffs assert that the Smithsonian holds its collection in constructive trust for the people of the United States or a subsection of U.S. citizens that descended from West Africa, the D.C. Circuit has held that only the United States holds legal title to the Smithsonian collection as its trustee. *Dong*, 125 F.3d at 883. Nor would it be appropriate for the Court to create a constructive trust over the Bronzes, as Plaintiffs request, because they have not alleged that they hold some property interest in the Bronzes that the Smithsonian obtained through improper means. *See U.S. v. Taylor*, 867 F.2d 700, 703 (D.C. Cir. 1989) ("Courts impose a constructive trust to redress the injustice that would otherwise occur when one person has fraudulently or wrongfully obtained the property of another.").

Plaintiffs' unjust enrichment claim suffers from a similar defect. Unjust enrichment occurs when a defendant receives a benefit from the plaintiff without providing adequate compensation for that benefit. *Rapaport v. Dep't of Treas.*, 59 F.3d 212, 217 (D.C. Cir. 1995). Here, Plaintiffs do not seek compensation for any benefit they bestowed on the Smithsonian. Rather, they seek to block the Smithsonian from voluntarily transferring property that it legally holds to a third-party. That does not fit the mold of an unjust enrichment claim.

Accordingly, Plaintiffs are not likely to prevail on any of their claims.

Plaintiffs also have not adequately alleged that they will suffer irreparable harm if a portion of the Smithsonian's collection of Benin Bronzes is transferred to Nigeria. First, at least some of the Bronzes will remain at the Museum of African Art for the foreseeable future. Compl. ¶ 65. Second, if Plaintiffs are interested in visiting the transferred Bronzes, they can do so by traveling from New York to Nigeria.[2] While that would be more expensive and inconvenient than seeing the Bronzes in Washington, D.C., such harms do not constitute irreparable injuries. *Chaplaincy of Full Gospel Churches v. England*, 454 F.3d 290, 297 (D.C. Cir. 2006) ("Mere injuries, however substantial, in terms of money, time and energy necessarily expended in the absence of [an injunction] are not enough." (quoting *Wis. Gas Co. v. FERC*, 758 F.2d 669, 674 (D.C. Cir. 1985))).

For all these reasons, Plaintiffs' [2] Emergency Motion for Temporary Restraining Order and Preliminary Injunction is hereby DENIED.[3]

SO ORDERED.

/s/ Christopher R. Cooper
United States District Judge

Date: 10/14/2022

---

[2] Plaintiffs suggest that the Bronzes may not be displayed publicly after they arrive in Nigeria. Pls.' Reply at 3-4. That suggestion is inconsistent with Plaintiffs' acknowledgement that the Bronzes will be entrusted to the Edo Museum of West African Art, Pls.' Mot. TRO at 1, and with the Court's understanding of the overall purpose of the transfer agreement.

[3] The government has also moved to dismiss the case. The Court will reserve judgment on that motion. Should Plaintiffs wish to press on following this ruling, they may respond to the government's motion to dismiss by either filing a supplemental opposition within the time allowed under the Local Rules or amending their complaint as of right.

App.13a

**ORDER DENYING PETITION
FOR REHEARING, U.S. COURT OF
APPEALS FOR THE D.C. CIRCUIT
(FEBRUARY 29, 2024)**

UNITED STATES COURT OF APPEALS
FOR THE DISTRICT OF COLUMBIA CIRCUIT

DEADRIA FARMER-PAELLMANN AND
RESTITUTION STUDY GROUP, INC.,

Appellants,

v.

SMITHSONIAN INSTITUTION,

Appellee.

No. 23-5196

1:22-cv-03048-CRC

Before: HENDERSON, CHILDS, and PAN,
Circuit Judges.

ORDER

Upon consideration of the petition for rehearing, it is

ORDERED that the petition be denied.

Per Curiam

App.14a

FOR THE COURT:

<u>Mark J. Langer</u>
Clerk

BY: <u>/s/ Daniel J. Reidy</u>
Deputy Clerk

App.15a

COMPLAINT
(OCTOBER 7, 2022)

UNITED STATES DISTRICT COURT
FOR THE DISTRICT OF COLUMBIA

DEADRIA FARMER-PAELLMANN
15 West 12th Street, 6G
New York, NY 10011,

and

RESTITUTION STUDY GROUP, INC.
15 West 12th Street, 6G
New York, NY 10011,

Plaintiffs,

v.

SMITHSONIAN INSTITUTION
Office of General Counsel
1000 Jefferson Drive, Room 302
Washington, DC 20560,

Defendant.

Civil Case No. 1:22-cv-3048

COMPLAINT

For their Complaint, by and through counsel, Plaintiffs allege as follows:

I. Summary of Action

1. This is a class action complaint alleging an anticipatory breach of trust. Plaintiffs seek exclusively equitable relief that includes, among other things, a preliminary and permanent injunction to prevent Defendant Smithsonian Institution from effecting its gifting to the Federal Republic of Nigeria's National Commission for Museums and Monuments ("NCMM") of 29 of 39 Benin Bronzes, which have an approximate value in excess of $200 million, that the Smithsonian Institution owns and possesses as trustee for the People of the United States.

2. The Smithsonian Institution is not only a trust instrumentality for all people of the United States, but it is or should be a common law trust for the thousands of citizens of the United States who are descended from West African peoples who lived in what is now called Nigeria, and whose lives and liberty were destroyed by the greed of royal Beni[1] traffickers, European slave traders, and European agriculturalists in North America.

A. The Benin Bronzes Are Not Merely Cultural Objects

3. The Benin Bronzes are not simply valuable *objets d'art:* they have a unique and special historical relationship to descendants of enslaved African-Americans whom Europeans forcibly brought to North America. Many, but not all, of these objects were crafted from metal ingots, melted down from a currency called manillas, that European slave traders paid to the oba

___

[1] "Benin" refers to the Kingdom of Benin; "Beni" refers to the people who populated the Kingdom of Benin.

(the Beni term for king) of the Kingdom of Benin, or to members of the Benin nobility, in exchange for abducted and enslaved neighboring non-Beni people.

4. The cultural importance of the Benin Bronzes to citizens of the United States who are descendants of enslaved Africans from Western Africa who were abductees of royal Benin trafickers (specifically, from parts of what is now the Federal Republic of Nigeria, including the Benin river, Aghway, Lagos, Onim, Oere, and Rio Forcados) cannot be monetized. They offer a rare opportunity for all Americans to engage with the actual currency that caused people to be kidnapped and separated them from their homelands, families, languages, and religions.

5. After buying abducted enslaved people from royal Beni traffickers, the European slave traders (primarily Portuguese, Dutch, French, and English slavers) forcibly transported them to Brazil, the Caribbean, mainland North America, and Europe to work for, and be subjected, to the wealth-building needs of plantation owners. Meanwhile, the royal Beni traffickers had craftsmen transform these copper-based ingots into what are now called the Benin Bronzes.

B. The dispersal of the Benin Bronzes

6. During a raid in early 1897 on Benin City, the British seized over 10,000 of what became known as the Benin Bronzes. The stolen Benin Bronzes were dispersed throughout the world and are scattered in 160 museums and private collections. The Smithsonian holds thirty-nine of them.

C. Defendant's Impending Action and Its Bracketed Story

7. On June 13, 2022, Defendant Smithsonian Institution's Board of Regents resolved to deaccession and transfer 29 of its 39 Benin Bronzes to the control of descendants of Beni royalty, whose ancestors were never enslaved but who kidnapped, enslaved, and trafficked other peoples to European slave-traders in exchange for the bronze and brass from which the Benin Bronzes were made.

8. In undertaking this purported "ethical" action of returning stolen property to its "rightful" owners — the descendants of the royal Beni traffickers — Defendant has expediently bracketed the story of the Benin Bronzes to have begun in 1897 and to end happily with transfer to Nigerian Africans on October 11, 2022.

D. Defendants Disregard the Complete Story

9. Defendant knows that its bracketed story of the Benin Bronzes is an incomplete "undoing" of European colonialists' and slavers' wrongs against Africans from the area now called Nigeria in the late 19th century: the Board of Regents knows or should know that the bigger theft was by European slave traders and royal Beni traffickers who stole thousands of people's lives and liberty so that Europeans could enhance agricultural profits without having to pay for labor and so royal Beni traffickers could obtain copper-based metal that they would fashion into iconic sculptures.

10. Only by means of this first and much more important theft—abductions and sales of innocent

people and the loss of their liberty and lives—could this wealth in metallic sculptures have been acquired for later theft by the British. This story actually began in the early 16th century and it has yet to end. It cannot be "undone" or ended by the expedient of returning to the traffickers the payments they received in exchange for sacrificing the lives of the ancestors of African-Americans of Nigerian descent.

11. Defendant's planned action assumes that Africans have a single and unified interest, but American Africans who originated in Western Africa have no interest in returning the payment that Beni royalty received from European slave-traders for having jointly trafficked them.

12. The Government of the United States has thwarted efforts to make any reparations to descendants of African enslaved people whose lives, liberty, and labor created immense wealth for certain elites in the United States. Return of the payments made for the lives, liberty, and labor of these abducted and enslaved people to the traffickers is the opposite of reparation: it is effectively a "thank you."

II. Parties

A. Defendant

13. <u>Smithsonian Institution.</u> The Smithsonian Institution is a non-profit entity created in 1846. Congress and President James Polk passed an Act to Establish Smithsonian Institution (9 Stat. 102) as a trust instrumentality of the United States ("Act of Establishment"), organized in the District of Columbia and created to hold in trust the assets of the British chemist and minerologist, James Smithson who

bequeathed them to the United States "for the increase and diffusion of knowledge among men."

14. The Act of Establishment assigned the Smithsonian Institution various roles and functions, including the roles of museum, observatory, library, laboratory, and depository for copyrights.

15. As a trust, the Board of Regents and the Secretary administer the Smithsonian Institution. On the June 10, 1857, the *Opinion of Attorney General* [Judge Jeremiah S. Black] *on National Museum* determined that the Smithsonian Institution was the National Museum and as such could receive appropriations from the national government to care for National Collections. Annual appropriations beginning in 1858.

B. Plaintiffs

16. <u>Deadria Farmer-Paellman.</u> Plaintiff Deadria Farmer-Paellmann, J.D., M.A. ("Farmer-Paellmann"), is a citizen and resident of the United States, domiciled in the State of New York, and is of Nigerian descent. Specifically, she descends in part from peoples located within the sphere of influence of the Kingdom of Benin, in Lagos and near Warri, the ports from which many people captured by the Beni were transshipped to the United States. She founded and incorporated Restitution Study Group, Inc. Her ancestors are likely abductees of royal Beni traffickers who sold them to European slave traders and who, as a result, were transported to and disembarked at communities near Charleston, South Carolina, the main port where Beni-trafficked enslaved people disembarked to be further sold into bondage.

17. <u>Restitution Study Group, Inc.</u> Plaintiff Restitution Study Group, Inc. ("RSG") is a New York non-profit corporation that Deadria Farmer-Paellmann founded on May 8, 2003, and is a tax-exempt corporation under the Internal Revenue Code, 26 U.S.C. 501(c)(3). Its purpose is to promote slavery justice, and its Web site is www.rsgincorp.org.

18. RSG was formed to "examine and execute innovative approaches to healing the injuries of exploited and oppressed people." It represents heirs to the treasures of the Benin Bronzes who are DNA descendants of enslaved people who financed the making of the relics with their lives and "partners with community advocates to bring about positive change through litigation, legislation, genealogy and DNA research, and direct action." RSG's Web site states:

> One of our primary efforts has been to secure reparations and restitution from corporations complicit in the antebellum enslavement of Africans. Our goal is to create a Community Trust Fund managed by Black business and community leaders to invest in efforts to repair the economic, educational, and health disparities from which descendants of enslaved Africans suffer.

19. <u>Class of DNA Descendants.</u> The proposed class includes all African-Americans who are citizens of the United States and whose ancestors were also residents of what is now called Nigeria whom royal Beni traffickers kidnapped and sold to European slave traders. Research shows that over 90% of United States citizens who are descendants of African enslaved people in the United States can trace their ancestry to

one of four Atlantic African populations, with the area that now forms the Repulic of Nigeria being the most common.

C. Other Relevant Persons

20. <u>Board of Regents.</u> Congress established a Board of Regents to administer the Smithsonian Institution, and its members include the Chief Justice of the United States, the Vice President of the United States, three members of the United States Senate, three members of the United States House of Representatives, and nine citizens. The Board of Regents meets at least four times each year and typically convenes in the Regents Room.

21. <u>Director of the National Museum of African Art.</u> The Smithsonian Institution displayed the Benin Bronzes in the National Museum of African Art, which Warren M. Robbins (1923-2008) founded in 1964 as the Museum of African Art ("MAfA"). Robbins wanted MAfA to be a private educational organization for providing "a foundation for interracial understanding," and later lobbied Congress to incorporate 'it into the Smithsonian Institution; in 1979, the MafA became part of the Smithsonian Institution, and 1981, the Smithsonian Institution renamed it the *National Museum of African Art* ("NMAA"). Ngaire Blankenberg is the Director of the NMAA.

III. Jurisdiction and Venue

A. Jurisdiction

22. This Court has jurisdiction of this action under 28 U.S.C. § 1331, because it involves a federal

question and the Defendant is an instrument or component of the United States Government.

23. This Court also has jurisdiction of this action under 28 U.S.C. § 1332, because Plaintiffs Farmer-Paellmann and RSG are domiciled in the State of New York and Defendant Smithsonian Institution is domiciled in the District of Columbia.

24. The judicial doctrine of sovereign immunity does not block the Court's jurisdiction because Plaintiffs are seeking exclusively equitable, non-monetary relief

25. This Court also has jurisdiction of this action under the Class Action Fairness Act, 28 U.S.C. § 1332(d). In this action: (1) the proposed class includes 100 or more members, namely, African-Americans of Nigerian descent; (2) the members of the proposed class include some who do not live in this district and have citizenship different from Defendant's citizenship; and (3) the claims of the proposed class members involve assets, namely, the Benin Bronzes, that exceed $5 million in aggregate value.

26. This Court also has supplemental jurisdiction under 28 U.S.C. § 1367 over Plaintiffs because the claims of this class derive from a common nucleus of operative fact.

27. This Court has personal jurisdiction over Defendant because it is domiciled in the District of Columbia, the Benin Bronzes are located in the District of Columbia, and many or all of the relevant actions and anticipated actions complained of herein and giving rise to the claims alleged herein have occurred and, unless prevented, will occur in this District.

B. Venue

Venue is proper in this District pursuant to 28 U.S.C. § 1391(b) because a substantial part of the events giving rise to the claims occurred in the District of Columbia.

IV. Standing of Plaintiffs

29. Defendant Smithsonian Institution holds the Benin Bronzes in the National Collection, which is the trust corpus, as: (1) the Trustee for the People of the United States, not only the Government of the United States, and (2) the Trustee of a special common law trust of the United States for United States citizens descended from that portion of Western Africa now called Nigeria whose ancestors the Kingdom of Benin abducted and sold—for the metals contained in Benin Bronzes produced from the 16th to 19th centuries—into Anglo-American slavery.

30. Plaintiffs have personal stakes in the outcome of this action insofar as the metal of which the Benin Bronzes are made *are* and *represent* monetary or in-kind metallic value that European slavers used to pay royal Beni traffickers for the lives and liberties of Plaintiffs' enslaved ancestors.

31. Defendant's planned relinquishment of the Benin Bronzes to the descendants of those who were essential in the trafficking of Plaintiff Farmer-Paellmann's and the Class's ancestors would cause yet another moral and economic injury to Plaintiffs that can be prevented only if the equitable relief sought herein is granted.

V. Plaintiffs' Exhaustion of Administrative Remedies

32. After learning on March 8, 2022, of Defendant's intention to deaccession and transfer the Benin Bronzes, particularly those fabricated during the 16th to 19th centuries when the transatlantic slave trade occurred, Plaintiffs Farmer-Paellmann and RSG sent an email on March 12, 2022, to the Director of the Smithsonian Institution's National Museum of African Art, ("NMAA") Ngaire Blankenberg ("NMAA Director"), explaining the origins of the Benin Bronzes and the harm that the Smithsonian Institution would cause in transferring them to Nigeria and requesting, among other things, that a trust be created for these artifacts.

33. On March 13, 2022, Plaintiffs sent a letter to the Director and Secretary of the Smithsonian Institution and its Board of Regents reiterating what Ms. Farmer-Paellmann wrote to Blankenberg.

34. On March 14, 2022, the NMAA Director proposed to arrange a meeting which took place on March 28, 2022. The NMAA Director and the Archivist of the NMAA indicated that they had no knowledge of the relationship between the Benin Bronzes and the transatlantic slave trade. The NMAA Director stated that she had the exclusive authority to transfer items unless the artifacts had a certain value.

35. After the meeting of March 28, 2022, Plaintiffs Farmer-Paellmann and RSG discovered that the Smithsonian Institution had written extensively on the Benin Bronzes, noting their role in the slave trade. For example, Defendant's own published article, entitled "The Royal Art of Benin: In the Collection of the National Museum of African Art (1987)," states:

The oba controlled foreign trade. While guns were desired imports, the trade currency was often the manilla, a C-shaped metal ingot that came in a range of sizes and weights. The bracelet like form on the base by the figures right heel is a variant of the standard shape. At first made of copper, most manillas were later made of brass. They were melted for use in art objects or worn as regalia. In 1517, a single ship brought thirteent thousand manillas. Fourty-five manillas were traded for an eighty pound tusk and fifty-seven for a slave (Ryder, 1969, 40, 53).

36. By April 20, 2022, Plaintiffs Farmer-Paellmann and RSG contacted the Inspector General of the Smithsonian Institution ("OIG") with the complaint that transferring the Benin Bronzes, so critical to the origin and history of slave-holding in the United States, could be fraud, waste, or abuse.

37. On April 21, 2022, a special agent of the OIG followed up by contacting Plaintiffs Farmer-Paellmann and indicated that an investigation had been opened. On May 4, Plaintiff Farmer-Paellmann placed a follow-up call to the OIG special agent, who provided no update on the status of the complaint.

38. On May 16, 2022, Plaintiffs Farmer-Paellmann and RSG sent references to scholarly works about the Benin Bronzes that discussed their linkage to the slave trade to the NMAA Director and requested an update on the status of the transfer. The NMAA Director responded the same day, by email that copied Defendant's Office of General Counsel ("OGC"), and expressed interest in working with RSG and its experts to develop future exhibits for the Benin Bronzes. The

NMAA Director did not update Plaintiffs on the status of the proposed transfer.

39. On May 23, 2022, Plaintiffs Farmer-Paellmann and RSG followed up by emailing the NMAA Director, copying the OGC, with the names and the contact information for RSG's historian, curator, and genealogist. They also requested Defendant's help in meeting with Nigerian officials to discuss the issue of co-ownership of the Benin Bronzes and noted that a third-party foundation had indicated that it would offer funds in the amount of $300 million to reach a resolution. The NMAA Director never replied.

40. On June 6, 2022, Plaintiffs Farmer-Paellmann and RSG placed a follow-up call to the OIG requesting an update. The OIG provided no update.

41. On June 15, 2022, two days after Smithsonian Institution announced the transfer of 29 of the 39 Benin Bronzes to Nigeria, Plaintiffs Farmer-Paellmann and RSG emailed the NMAA Director, copying the OGC, and posed four questions: (1) Will the Smithsonian Institution grant co-ownership of the Benin Bronzes to DNA descendants? (2) Did the Board of Regents receive the proof of the slave-trade origin of the Benin Bronzes before resolving to transfer them? (3) What will become of the ten Benin Bronzes not being transferred to Nigeria? and (4) When will the meetings start to plan future exhibits?

42. On July 5, 2022, Plaintiffs Farmer-Paellmann and RSG followed up by email and telephone with the OIG and received, again, no response.

43. On July 6, 2022, Plaintiffs Farmer-Paellmann and RSG placed a follow-up telephone call with the

OIG special agent who told them that there was no update.

44. On July 15, 2022, Plaintiffs Farmer-Paellmann and RSG followed up by email and telephone with the OIG's special agent and received, again, no response.

45. On July 19, 2022, OIG's special agent informed Plaintiffs Farmer-Paellmann and RSG that the matter had been referred to OGC and provided a telephone number for OGC. Plaintiffs called that number, left a message, and never received a response.

46. On July 28, 2022, the NMAA Director responded by email, copying the OGC, to Plaintiffs Farmer-Paellmann and RSG's email of June 15, 2022, in which she represented that (1) the Smithsonian Institution would let Plaintiffs know when they would be needed for exhibit planning; (2) the transfer of the Benin Bronzes will be exclusively to Nigeria's National Commission of Museums and Monuments; (3) more research was needed to link Defendant's Benin Bronzes to the transatlantic slave trade and to determine that they were made from payments of manillas for humans; (4) the role of the Kingdom of Benin in the slave trade is "less documented" than that of other African Kingdoms; and (5) the Kingdom of Benin's role in slavery appeared to be the subject of a misinformation campaign.

47. On July 29, 2022, Plaintiffs Farmer-Paellmann and RSG's emailed the OIG special agent requesting another means to contact the OGC, and he provided an email address.

48. On September 27, 2022, the day after the Smithsonian Institution announced that the Benin Bronzes would be transferred to Nigeria on October 11, Plaintiff Farmer-Paellmann telephoned the OGC

and left a message. She received no response. She called again on September 29 and again received no response. The same day, Plaintiff Farmer-Paellmann sent a follow-up email to Craig Blackwell, a member of the OGC staff who had been copied on all of Blankenberg's emails on and after May 16, 2022, and he did not respond.

49. On the afternoon of October 6, 2022, Kevin Gover of the Smithsonian Institution emailed Plaintiff Farmer-Paellmann, stating:

> I am the Undersecretary for Museums and Culture at the Smithsonian Institution. This message responds to your inquiry about "what has the Smithsonian decided to do with the Benin Bronzes?" In April 2022, the Smithsonian adopted a policy on ethical returns. Pursuant to the process provided under that policy and the National Museum of African Art's collections management policy, it was decided that certain Benin bronzes in the collections of the Smithsonian be deaccessioned. Those deaccessioned items will be returned to the Federal Government of Nigeria, through its National Commission for Museums and Monuments.
>
> We know that you have a different perspective regarding to whom these works should be returned. While we understand your position, the Smithsonian has made its decision, and that decision is consistent with our policy and reflects the best judgment of our museum professionals and others charged with management and stewardship of our collections.

App.30a

50. The October 6, 2022, email from Mr. Gover apparently represents Defendant Smithsonian Institution's final decision in its administrative process.

VI. Allegations of Fact

A. The Complete Story of the Benin Bronzes

51. The Benin Bronzes are a collection of iconic sculptures casted from copper alloys, including brass and bronze. Specialist guilds working for the Royal Court of the oba (king) of Benin City used the oba's metal wealth to make them.

52. The Benin royalty practice of using metals and other materials, including elephant tusks, for fabrication into iconic sculptures began no later than the 11th century C.E. and continued through the 19th century C.E. The West Africans developed a tradition of casting brass sculptures that dates to the medieval period.

B. European Payment of Benin Traffickers in Bronze Ingots (Manillas)

53. Beginning in the early 1500s, the capitals and courts of the Kingdoms of Benin and Portugal developed diplomatic relations, through emissaries, and established trade relations.

54. The Portugese and subsequent European traders thereafter began contracting with the Kingdom of Benin and its King (Oba) to supply West Africans for transport to the North and South American continents to work as enslaved people for Europeans.

55. The royal Beni performed these supply contracts by abducting residents of West Africa, including

from parts of the area now called Nigeria, and delivering them to European slavers in exchange for the metal (copper) currency called manillas.

C. Benin Traffickers Crafted the Manillas into the Benin Bronzes

56. Upon receiving the manillas, the Oba and royal Beni had metalsmiths and craftsmen melt the manillas and cast the metals into iconic sculptures now called the Benin Bronzes. Those Benin Bronzes crafted from the 16th to the 19th centuries were made from manillas that royal Benin traffickers had received as payment for the West Africans they had kidnapped and sold to Europeans.

D. The British Seize the Benin Bronzes

57. British colonial expansion in the 19th century led to a clash with the Kingdom of Benin. The British gradually expanded into land around the kingdom and an increasing reluctance to accept Benin's trading conditions created an atmosphere of distrust and animosity.

58. In January 1897, Nigerians attacked officers of the Royal Navy and African porters on a "trade mission" to Benin City and killed seven British delegates and 230 porters. The British retaliated by sending a military expedition against the Kingdom of Benin.

59. In February 1897, British forces captured Benin City.

60. In the raid and capture of Benin City, the British seized and removed the Benin Bronzes from Nigeria, and incorporated Benin City into its Empire, where it remained from 1897 to 1960.

E. Dispersal of the Benin Bronzes

61. After looting the Benin Bronzes, the Benin Bronzes were disbursed. Many, some 900, are in the British Museum. The Museum's Web site notes:

> Many pieces were commissioned specifically for the ancestral altars of past Obas [Kings] and Queen Mothers. They were also used in other rituals to honour the ancestors and to validate the accession of a new Oba. Among the most well-known of the Benin Bronzes are the cast brass plaques which once decorated the Benin royal palace and which provide an important historical record of the Kingdom of Benin.

62. The estimated value of the Benin Bronzes ranges from $20,000,000,000 to $30,000,000,000.

F. Defendant Smithsonian Institution's Receipt of 39 Benin Bronzes

63. After 1897, Defendant Smithsonian Institution acquired at least 39 of the Benin Bronzes.

G. Defendant's Resolution to Deaccession and Transfer the Benin Bronzes

64. Beginning in March 2022, several European countries considered and undertook to repatriate their Benin Bronzes to Nigeria, apparently in an effort to undo the colonial wrongs of the 19th century.

65. On June 13, 2022, the Smithsonian Board of Regents voted to de-accession twenty-nine (29) of Defendant's thirty-nine (39) Benin Bronzes and officially remove the Benin Bronzes from its holdings and transfer them to Nigeria.

66. Defendant Smithsonian Institution noted that it would execute a memorandum of understanding ("MOU") with the National Commission for Museums and Monuments of the Federal Republic of Nigeria to create educational programs, and photography and digital workshops for artists, children and educators.

67. On September 26, 2022, the Smithsonian Board of Regents voted to de-accession the twenty-nine (29) Benin Bronzes and officially remove the Benin Bronzes from its listed holdings and to repatriate them to Nigeria on October 11, 2022.

68. On October 4, 2022, Plaintiffs Farmer-Paellmann and RSG retained counsel to seek to enjoin Defendant from deaccessioning the twenty-nine (29) Benin Bronzes and transferring them to Nigeria on October 11, 2022.

COUNT I
ACTING WITHOUT STATUTORY AUTHORITY

69. Plaintiffs repeat and reallege each and every allegation of Paragraphs 1 through 68 above as though fully set forth herein.

70. Defendant Smithsonian Institution lacks the statutory authority under Title 20 of the United States Code to transfer assets of the National Museum of African American Art to third parties without consideration.

71. The authority under 20 U.S.C. § 80q-9 to repatriate Native American "cultural patrimony" objects does not extend to repatriation of cultural objects to Nigeria.

72. Defendant's upcoming transfer of the Benin Bronzes is *ultra vices* and unauthorized.

COUNT II
ANTICIPATORY BREACH OF TRUST TO THE PEOPLE OF THE UNITED STATES

73. Plaintiffs repeat and reallege each and every allegation of Paragraphs 1 through 68 above as though fully set forth herein.

74. Defendant Smithsonian Institution is a trust instrumentality of the United States ("Trust"), which consists of its citizens.

75. Assets of the Smithsonian Institution, the National Collection, make up the Corpus of the Trust and include the Benin Bronzes.

76. Defendant Smithsonian Institution acts as Trustee for the People of the United States, namely, the citizens of the United States who are the beneficiaries of the National Collection.

77. As Trustee, the Smithsonian Institution has a fiduciary duty to the citizens of the United States.

78. Defendant Smithsonian Institution's planned transfer of the Benin Bronzes made during the trafficking and enslavement period from the 16th to 19th centuries would breach its fiduciary duty to Plaintiffs and those similarly situated insofar as it would be dissipating invaluable Trust assets that are culturally invaluable and irreplaceable.

79. Plaintiffs would suffer damages, emotionally and potentially economically, from Defendant Smithsonian Institution's breach of fiduciary duty in transferring the Benin Bronzes to Nigeria.

80. Defendant Smithsonian Institution's breach of its fiduciary duty to the descendants of slave traffickers would cause Plaintiffs damages.

COUNT III
ANTICIPATORY BREACH OF TRUST TO UNITED STATES CITIZENS DESCENDED FROM WEST AFRICANS TRAFFICKED BY BENIN ROYALTY

81. Plaintiffs repeat and reallege each and every allegation of Paragraphs 1 through 68 above as though fully set forth herein.

82. The Benin Bronzes made from copper and copper alloys that Europeans paid to royal Beni traffickers for West African enslaved people that are in the possession of Defendant Smithsonian Institution constitute payment for ancestors of many thousands of United States citizens.

83. These Benin Bronzes are central to the Smithsonian's core activities of scholarship, discovery, exhibition, and education and are a vital resource that constitute or should constitute a common law trust for the benefit of descendants of West Africans whom royal Beni traffickers and European slave-traders kidnaped and enslaved.

84. Metallurgical experts can verify the European origin of the copper alloys present in the Benin Bronzes made with manillas from the Portuguese and other subsequent European slave traders for purposes of identifying the specific Benin Bronzes made from manillas used to pay for kidnaped West Africans.

85. Defendant Smithsonian Institution acts as Trustee for the citizens of the United States who are

descendants of those enslaved by royal Benin traffickers.

86. As Trustee, the Smithsonian Institution has a fiduciary duty to the citizens of the United States.

87. Defendant Smithsonian Institution's planned transfer of the Benin Bronzes made during the trafficking and enslavement period from the 16th to 19th centuries would breach its fiduciary duty to Plaintiffs and those similarly situated insofar as it would be dissipating invaluable Trust assets that are culturally invaluable and irreplaceable.

88. Plaintiffs would suffer damages, emotionally and potentially economically, from Defendant Smithsonian Institution's breach of fiduciary duty in transferring the Benin Bronzes to Nigeria.

89. Defendant Smithsonian Institution's breach of its fiduciary duty to the descendants of slave traffickers would cause Plaintiffs damages.

COUNT IV
UNJUST ENRICHMENT

90. Plaintiffs repeat and reallege each and every allegation of Paragraphs 1 through 68 above as though fully set forth herein.

91. Defendant Smithsonian Institution has no contractual obligations to transfer its Benin Bronzes to descendants of Beni, Nigerians, or other West Africans responsible for having enslaved American-Africans.

92. Citizens of the British North American colonies and citizens of the United States built enormous wealth from the unpaid labor of enslaved

West Africans, including the many whom royal Beni traffickers abducted and sold to slave-traders for manillas.

93. The sale-and-purchase transactions between American slave-holders, European slave-traders, and royal Beni traffickers enriched all three groups at the exclusive expense of the West Africans and their descendants who were forced into enslavement.

94. If Defendant Smithsonian Institution "gifts" the Benin Bronzes to the royal Beni traffickers, it would be an agent of (1) the unjust enrichment of those who engaged in all-too-common crimes against humanity, without receipt of any compensation; and (2) the unjust impoverishment of those whose lives were lost and destroyed for such metals and the objects fashioned therefrom.

95. On the grounds of fairness and justice, Defendant Smithsonian Institution has a moral and legal obligation to not enrich descendants of those with the assets they obtained through their brutality of kidnapping and trafficking human beings.

96. Paying descendants of human traffickers with the fruits of their vile transactions is a statement that condones such conduct and is offensive to the many thousands of United States citizens of West African descent whose ancestors suffered savage treatment as enslaved people in North America.

PRAYER FOR RELIEF

As and for relief, Plaintiffs respectfully request that the Court:

App.38a

1. Order that Defendant Smithsonian Institution be permanently enjoined from transferring title to those Benin Bronzes that were fabricated from the 16th century to the 19th century and that were made from metals traded to the Kingdom of Benin in exchange for enslaved people of Western Africa; and

2. Grant such other and further relief as the Court deems appropriate.

/s/ Adriaen M. Morse
Adriaen M. Morse (D.C. Bar No. 483347)
Cory Kirchert (D.C. Bar No. Pending)
Lionel Andre (D.C. Bar No. 422534)
SECIL LAW PLLC
1701 Pennsylvania Avenue, NW, Suite 200
Washington, D.C. 20006
Tel: 202.417.8232
amorse@secillaw.com

Counsel for Plaintiffs

Dated: October 7, 2022

App.39a

EMERGENCY MOTION FOR TRO AND PRELIMINARY INJUNCTION
(OCTOBER 7, 2022)

UNITED STATES DISTRICT COURT
FOR THE DISTRICT OF COLUMBIA

DEADRIA FARMER-PAELLMANN and RESTITUTION STUDY GROUP, on behalf of themselves and all others similarly situated,

Plaintiffs,

v.

SMITHSONIAN INSTITUTION,

Defendant.

Civil Action No. 1:22-cv-3048

ORAL ARGUMENT REQUESTED

PLAINTIFFS' EMERGENCY MOTION FOR EMERGENCY TEMPORARY RESTRAINING ORDER AND PRELIMINARY INJUNCTION

Pursuant to Fed. R. Civ. P. 65 and LCvR 65.1, Plaintiffs, by and through undersigned counsel, hereby move the Court for a Temporary Restraining Order and Preliminary Injunction enjoining Defendant, the Smithsonian Institution, a trust instrumentality of the United States, from deaccessioning and transferring from its collection certain works of art known as the "Benin Bronzes," which Defendant is planning to

App.40a

formally transfer to Nigeria's National Commission for Museums and Monuments in a private ceremony on October 11, 2022. Plaintiffs have exhausted any other administrative remedies available to them through the Smithsonian Institution's administrative process.

An emergency hearing is essential in order for the Court to consider and rule on the requested injunctive relief and Plaintiffs request an order to be issued to Defendant forbidding the transfer of the Benin Bronzes on October 11 and until such time as the Court has ruled on the merits of this case.

In support of this motion, Plaintiffs rely upon the attached memorandum of points and authorities. A proposed order is attached. Oral argument is respectfully requested.

/s/ Adriaen M. Morse
Adriaen M. Morse (D.C. Bar No. 483347)
Cory Kirchert (D.C. Bar No. Pending)
Lionel Andre (D.C. Bar No. 422534)
SECIL LAW PLLC
1701 Pennsylvania Avenue, NW, Suite 200
Washington, D.C. 20006
Tel: 202.417.8232
amorse@secillaw.com

Counsel for Plaintiffs

Dated: October 7, 2022

CONTRACT BETWEEN SMITHSONIAN INSTITUTION AND NIGERIAN NATIONAL COMMISSION FOR MUSEUMS AND MONUMENTS (OCTOBER 11, 2022)

SMITHSONIAN NATIONAL MUSEUM OF AFRICAN ART

Agreement Between the Smithsonian Institution, Through Its National Museum of African Art, and the Nigerian National Commission for Museums and Monuments, on Behalf of the Federal Government of Nigerian

This Agreement ("Agreement"), effective as of the date of the last Party to sign below ("Effective Date"), is between the Smithsonian Institution ("Smithsonian"), a trust instrumentality of the United States, through its National Museum of African Art ("NMAfA"), having its principal place of business at 950 Independence Avenue, SW, Washington, DC, 20560, and the Federal Government of Nigeria, through its National Commission for Museums and Monuments ("NCMM"), having its principal place of business at Federal Secretariat Complex, Block C, Central Business District, Shehu Shagari Way, P.M.B. 171 Garki, Abuja, Nigeria (collectively "the Parties")

WHEREAS, NMAfA contacted NCMM in October 2021 to discuss the potential transfer of certain works of Benin Kingdom court arts, known as Benin Bronzes, in NMAfA's collection tied to the raid of the Benin Kingdom conducted by the British in February 1897;

WHEREAS, NCMM submitted a written request to the Smithsonian by email dated January 12, 2022, formally seeking the transfer of these Benin Bronzes;

WHEREAS, NMAfA has conducted extensive provenance research into the Benin Bronzes in its collection and has determined that twenty-nine (29) of the Benin Bronzes were, or likely were, removed in the 1897 raid ("the 29 Benin Bronzes," itemized on Appendix A);

WHEREAS, NMAfA is continuing to research six (6) Benin Bronzes in its collection that possibly were removed in the 1897 raid ("the 6 Benin Bronzes"), and is seeking NCMM's assistance in this effort;

WHEREAS, NMAfA wishes to transfer title immediately in the 29 Benin Bronzes to NCMM, as a representative of the Federal Government of Nigeria, and NCMM wishes to receive title to these art works;

WHEREAS, NMAfA and NCMM have a history of collaboration and wish to engage in activities that would further their shared goal of exchanging knowledge of their respective collections, lending, exhibiting and commissioning arts of Nigeria, and undertaking projects related to education, art, culture, history and similar activities related to arts from the Royal Kingdom of Benin, the Edo State and Nigeria as a whole;

NOW THEREFORE, NMAfA and NCMM agree as follows:

1. Ethical Return of the 29 Benin Bronzes.

    a. NMAfA hereby transfers all of its right and title in and to the 29 Benin Bronzes itemized on Appendix A to NCMM, on behalf of the Federal Government of Nigeria.

    b. NMAfA will pay the costs of packing and shipping the Benin Bronzes to NCMM at Abuja Airport. Any Benin Bronzes loaned by NCMM to NMAfA under Paragraph 3 below will be physically returned to NCMM at the end of the loan period in accordance with the loan agreement. All other Benin Bronzes will be physically returned to NCMM within 14 days of the Effective Date of this Agreement. Prior to returning any of the 29 Benin Bronzes, NMAfA will prepare a condition report prior to packing the object(s) and will provide the condition report to NCMM.

    c. As of the Effective Date of this Agreement, NCMM bears sole responsibility for the 29 Benin Bronzes, including sole responsibility for any damage to or loss of the 29 Benin Bronzes, and NMAfA will bear no responsibility for the 29 Benin Bronzes, with the sole exception that NMAfA will insure the 29 Benin Bronzes until they are received by NCMM at the address specified in ¶ 1.b above, or, for loaned objects, at the address specified in the loan agreement, including during any period when one or more of the 29 Benin Bronzes are on loan to NMAfA prior to being received by NCMM at the specified address.

1. During any period when NMAfA is required to insure the Benin Bronzes under this Agreement, NMAfA will insure the works under its fine-arts policy for the amounts stated on Appendix A against all risk of physical loss or damage from any external cause while in transit and on location during the period of any loan. NMAfA's fine-arts policy contains exclusions for loss or damage due to war, invasion, hostilities, rebellion, insurrection, confiscation by order of any Government or public authority, risks of contraband or illegal transportation and/or trade, nuclear damage, wear and tear, gradual deterioration, insects, vermin, and inherent vice, and for damage sustained due to and resulting from any repairing, restoration, or re-touching. NCMM must notify NMAfA within ten (10) days of receipt of any damage to or loss of any of the 29 Benin Bronzes.

2. In the event of loss, damage or theft during any period when NMAfA is required to insure the Benin Bronzes under this Agreement, recovery by NCMM shall be limited to such amount, if any, as may be paid by the insurer, and NCMM hereby releases the United States, and the Smithsonian and NMAfA and their Regents, officers, employees, and agents, from liability for any and all

claims arising out of such loss or damage. Any recovery for depreciation or loss of value shall be calculated as a percentage of the insured value agreed upon by the Parties. NCMM agrees to accept renumeration in U.S. Currency.

d. As of the Effective Date, NCMM, on behalf of the Federal Government of Nigeria, hereby releases and holds harmless the United States, and the Smithsonian and NMAfA and their Regents, officers, employees, and agents, from any third-party claims, disputes, lawsuits, or other proceedings arising from the return of the Benin Bronzes including, without limitation, claims by individuals, families, groups, rulers, or governments, alleging that they have an interest in the Benin Bronzes superior to the interests of NCMM or the Federal Government of Nigeria.

2. <u>Photography and 3-D Scanning</u>. Prior to physically returning the 29 Benin Bronzes, NMAfA will digitally photograph and make 3D scans of the Bronzes. NMAfA will provide NCMM with these high-resolution digital images, 3D scans, and associated metadata for NCMM's use without restriction. NMAfA will retain copies of the digital photographs, 3D scans, and associated metadata in its archives for internal use by Smithsonian staff, but NMAfA will not otherwise use these photographs or 3D scans without NCMM's prior written permission. For purposes of obtaining such permission, NMAfA will contact: [ADD NCMM CONTACT].

3. <u>Loan of Benin Bronzes</u>. NCMM agrees to lend NMAfA nine (9) of the 29 Benin Bronzes for a period of five (5) years, subject to renewal for further terms upon the agreement of the Parties. The nine (9) artworks for loan are set forth in Appendix B. The loaned objects will be displayed at NMAfA and will represent Edo history and culture to NMAfA's visitors in its galleries in Washington, D.C., further demonstrating the strength and effectiveness of the NCMM-NMAfA collaboration to audiences in the United States. All credit lines and interpretative material associated with these works will be determined in consultation with NCMM and will reflect NCMM as the owner and lender of the works on display. The terms and conditions of the loan will be set forth in a separate loan agreement between the Parties. As acknowledgement of the Parties' shared strategic goals, NCMM agrees to waive any potential loan fees for lending these works to NMAfA.

4. <u>Other Collaborations</u>. The Parties entered into a Memorandum of Understanding effective August 5, 2022, to set forth their intentions with respect to other areas of collaborations, including:

   a. <u>Updating Records and Documentation</u>. NMAfA and NCMM staff desire to work collaboratively to develop and share knowledge and provenance information, and revise and update records and documentation, to better reflect the stories and context of the Benin Bronzes from a Benin-Edo perspective. This information will be reflected in all exhibitions and documentation of the Bronzes loaned by

NMAFA from the NCMM or included in any joint exhibition.

b. <u>Benin Today</u>. NMAfA and NCMM intend to work collaboratively to create a joint exhibition tentatively entitled *Benin Today* to open in 2023-2024 at either the National Museum of African Art in Washington D.C., the National Museum of Benin, or another appropriate venue as decided by the Parties. The exhibit will feature new artworks by Benin-Edo artists, created in response to the return of the Benin Bronzes.

c. <u>Educational Programming</u>. NCMM, NMAfA educators, and local artists desire to work together to produce innovative educational programs, workshops and seminars on Benin arts and photography for secondary and tertiary students, educators, emerging artists, curators, musicians, designers, makers and others.

d. <u>Conservation</u>. Building on their collective knowledge, skills, training and experience, NCMM and NMAfA staff intend to develop protocols relating to collection, documentation, exhibition, preservation and storage of the Benin Bronzes.

e. <u>Provenance Research on the 6 Benin Bronzes</u>. NCMM will assist NMAfA in continuing to research the 6 Benin Bronzes in NMAfA's collection that possibly were removed in the 1897 raid.

5. <u>Representatives</u>. The following individuals will serve as the day-to-day representatives of the Parties for purposes of implementing this Agreement, but shall have no authority under Paragraph 12 below to modify or change the Agreement.

For Smithsonian:

Ngaire Blankenberg
Director, National Museum of African Art
Smithsonian Institution BlankbergN@si.edu
(202) 633-4602

For NCMM:

Professor Abba Isa Tijani, Director General
National Commission for Museums and Monuments NCMM

Federal Secretariat Complex, Block C, Central Business District,

Shehu Shagari Way, P.M.B. 171 Garki, Abuja, Nigeria

6. <u>Confidentiality</u>. In consideration of the public nature of the Smithsonian, this Agreement will not be treated as confidential. In accordance with Smithsonian policy, this Agreement may be released if requested by organizations or individuals in a manner consistent with Smithsonian policy or applicable laws.

7. <u>Funding</u>. This Agreement creates no financial obligation or commitment of staff resources on the part of either Party except as expressly set forth herein.

8. <u>Relationship of the Parties</u>. Under no circumstances will this Agreement be construed as creating or establishing any formal, legal, association, partnership, joint venture, principal/agent or master/servant relationship between the Parties.

9. <u>Assignment</u>. This Agreement may not be assigned by either Party.

10. <u>Dispute Resolution</u>. Any dispute arising under this Agreement will be resolved in good faith by consultation or negotiation or by any other way mutually agreed between the Parties.

11. <u>Official Language</u>. The official language of this Agreement is English, which shall be the controlling language for all matters relating to the meaning or interpretation of this Agreement.

12. <u>Modification and Waivers</u>. No variation, amendment, change, modification or waiver of any term, provision or condition of this Agreement will be valid unless in writing and signed by the Authorized Representatives of both Parties.

13. <u>Entire Agreement</u>. The terms and conditions herein constitute the entire agreement and understanding by and between the Parties and shall supersede all other communications, negotiations, arrangements, and agreements either oral or written, with respect to the subject matter herein.

14. <u>Counterparts: Signatures</u>. This Agreement may be executed in duplicate and each original shall be equally effective. Signatures on this Agreement sent by facsimile or pdf are valid and binding as original signatures.

WE, THE UNDERSIGNED AUTHORIZED REPRESENTATIVES OF THE PARTIES, HAVE READ AND AGREE WITH THIS AGREEMENT:

NIGERIAN NATIONAL COMMISSION FOR MUSEUMS AND MONUMENS

By:

/s/ Professor Abba Isa Tijani
Director General

October 11, 2022

/s/ Barrister Babatunde Emmanuel Adebiyi
Director of Legal

October 11, 2022

THE SMITHSONIAN INSTITUTION

By:

/s/ Lonnie G. Bunch III
Secretary of the Smithsonian Institution

October 11, 2022

/s/ Ngaire Blankenberg
Director, National Museum of African Art

October 11, 2022

www.ingramcontent.com/pod-product-compliance
Lightning Source LLC
Chambersburg PA
CBHW082240220526
45479CB00005B/1291